Life
Derailed

By

Christina S. Cernik

PublishAmerica
Baltimore

First printing

PublishAmerica has allowed this work to remain exactly as the author intended, verbatim, without editorial input.

ISBN: 978-1-61582-888-3
PUBLISHED BY PUBLISHAMERICA, LLLP
www.publishamerica.com
Baltimore

Printed in the United States of America

A Special Thanks To:
Andrea Carlson

Story is based on actual events.
Names of the characters have been changed to protect their identity.

Dedication

To all the mothers seeking help from their addiction.
May they continue to have faith.

In All His Glory, This is for You Lord.

To my parents and family who have supported me and loved me through thick and thin. To my children who are my greatest inspiration and to my husband Doug for loving me for who I am.

Prologue

O h God, are you there? I'm down this road again. I can't believe I'm doing this, just get me home safe. This is crazy. I'm crazy for walking down the middle of Des Moines Memorial Drive in Seattle at four o'clock in the morning. As soon as I see headlights I'll jump back onto the sidewalk. I hate those bushes, feel like someone's going to jump out and grab me. Least this way I can see who's out there while walking in the middle of the damn road. So far so good. I wish Rocky didn't have to work in the morning, I know he had to go to sleep but I hate leaving while I still had some stash. It makes my walk home longer. Besides, I hate doing it at my parents' house. Damn wind, won't let me light my glass. Stopping is not an option, keep moving and just get home....

Chapter 1

My life is a vicious cycle but I can't stop it. When I try to be straight it only lasts for three days at the most. Not good enough. Not long enough to make any difference but at least my kids see me. I can cook and do their laundry while I'm home. I've been trying to get my feet on the ground ever since I got a divorce and moved back into my parents' house in Seattle. I hoped my life would turn around since I left the one fixation that kept me in my upside down world. Married with a man I loved and would do anything for, even lie for, steal and take the blame for when things went array. The divorce came after trying three times before to make our marriage work.

When I left Boise in 1996 I was at my worst. So I thought. The status of my addiction progressed and hitting bottom was repeated over and over again. My bottom after ten years this time around consisted of several things. Not a single episode was the epitome of bottoms, but rather the combination of several events contributed to my downfall.

Within three months my life had come crashing down on me. And for some reason I knew that I was being punished for going back on my promise that I had made to God, to be drug free. Every time I relapsed, things would happen in the worst way. Call it karma, call it fate. I called it punishment.

While living in Boise, Idaho things started when my husband and I had a fight and things escalated. I had called 911 but hung up. Police in turn called back and asked if things were ok. I said yes, but later in the evening the Police came to check up on me and the boys. According to the Police someone had called them out of concern, possibly a family member to make sure my kids and I were safe. When the police questioned my husband he admitted to something he shouldn't have and the police took it upon themselves to press charges. I didn't want Russ to go to jail but they wouldn't let me contest it and my boys saw their dad handcuffed and sent away. Russ remained in jail for a month.

In the meantime my addiction took off and the boys were sent to Ohio, again. Ohio is where my husband's family lived. Without the kids, I had so much free time and no obligations except for work, I became insidious. I had no care in the world. Soon things caught up with me. Two days before my divorce was final I lost my job as a Manager at Denny's. With that said, my husband gained full custody of my boys, despite their dad just getting out of jail with no job and a place to live. I was confused and didn't understand the decision the Judge made. I didn't know how to fight it either, I was just in shock. At the end, Russ said it didn't matter. I could have the kids live with me regardless of the Judges' decision.

It's a good thing we didn't have any more kids as irresponsible as we were but it didn't justify the abortion we had. We couldn't bring in another child in a broken home such as ours. I was twelve weeks along before I decided to abort and we were already separated so it was easier to make that decision. Russ didn't want to, but I was using again and couldn't chance it a third time.

Life wasn't worth living after all this happened to me all within three months. It was too much to handle and no reprieve in sight. And it didn't end there. The final straw that broke the camel's back was being evicted from my apartment and ended up living with an IV user cranked out all the time. I wanted to die and I attempted to commit suicide one time. Something prevented me from killing myself that day when I came across a church in route. God's presence filled me and I can hear a voice telling me to hang on. I didn't know what to hang to or where the voice came from but I didn't kill myself like I set out to do. I knew it was a sin to commit suicide but I was at the end of my rope. I was ashamed to ask God forgiveness. I was ashamed of myself. My oldest sister Rose asked me to move to Hawaii where she lived to get away from it all. Foolishly, I declined.

Once I got to my parents house, I tapped on Cord's window because I still didn't have a key to get in. "Let me in Cord," man that boy sleeps like a rock. "Cord!"

Tap, tap, tap. Finally, I got off the cat walk and jumped down to the front porch. I can hear him turning off the alarm and unlocking the door.

"Thanks baby," as I kissed him on the head and turned to lock the door once again.

I know the reason why my parents haven't given me a key. They didn't want me coming and going at all hours of the night. With a key it was harder for them to hear if I had left. I'd have to ring the doorbell when I got home to get in. In my room downstairs I fixed to finish off the rest of my stash and hopefully doze off for awhile before I had to get up again. Only thing is, I take too damn long to finish off just one rock. Some people smoke the whole thing in just two hits maybe even one! Not me, I crumble mine up and take small tokes. I'm always afraid of taking too big of a hit, much less take one and then blow my heart up. I don't like the thought of being found dead in a room of my parent's house.

"What do you want to eat Cord?" I asked my son, while I walked up the stairs with Isabelle.

"I already ate cereal, three bowls. Can I feed Isabelle?" as he was putting his bowl in the sink.

"Don't leave that bowl in the sink, wash it. No, I have something special for her to eat today unless you want to make the scrambled eggs?" I put Isabelle in her chair and kissed her on the forehead.

"Nay, never mind. You gonna have scrambled eggs Isabelle?" Turning his attention to his sister and tickling her feet, which were dangling from underneath the high-chair. What a nice thing to see, now that's what life's about, giggles. Cord turned and was about to run down the stairs, "Hey, your bowl!"

"I'm going to D's" and out he went. Damn kid.

My parents went to church this morning and haven't gotten back yet. I was lying in bed waiting for my parents to return so that I could go to sleep but I could hear Isabelle waking up next door to my room. I was tired, didn't get to bed till about 8:00, hell I don't think I even fell asleep, was too damn wired. But here I am now, in the kitchen cooking without an ounce of sleep.

Eleven thirty, wonder where my parents went. Isabelle was happy eating with her hands and I was pleasantly smiling at her. What a beautiful baby. She's so lucky I wasn't doing drugs while I was pregnant with her, unlike her brothers. I hated myself every second, every hit, every time I used while I was pregnant with the boys. Especially Cord. Thank God I did my novena with Cord. It was his only saving grace. As much as I was doing drugs he should have been addicted. Instead, he's a healthy strong boy and smarter than his peers. He's a miracle baby. He shouldn't have been so perfect. I smoked crack throughout my entire pregnancy with Cord, up to two weeks prior to him being born.

Just then Cord came walking in. Good, I needed to get cleaned up before my parents get back. "I'm going to take a shower Cord, watch your sister please."

Taking a shower was about the only time I could cry and no one would notice my tears or hear me. I hate my life but I love my kids and would never leave them without a mother. At least I'm alive, for now. Over and over again I beg, I pray and I cry to do the right thing. Frustrated and pissed at myself every time I come down off that shit. But then in the back of my head I'm plotting my next move to get back out. Damn it, I can't wait too long I need another hit. Slow down Chris, spend some time with your kids, clean the house a little and visit with your parents. That should appease them for awhile and get me till at least bed time before I make a move to leave again.

When I got out of the shower I can hear my parents and a lot of noise going on. They're finally home and by the sound of it I think they went to Costco again. They spend so much money on food for us. Cupboards are always full. I know my kids will never go hungry living here and they will always be cared for. I don't know what I would do without my folks. I know I've hurt them numerous times and no matter what they won't turn the other cheek on me. Just last week I had to stop my mom from crying so hard. It was a cry of mourning, like someone had died. I never heard that come from my mom before. And her eyes, I will never forget her eyes. So much pain, hurt, disappointment and fear all bundled up in her brown tired eyes. I'm the cause of that look and it kills me. I held her tight and I swore under my breath that I was going to make things right for myself and for my kids some day. If it was the last thing I do, I wasn't going to be like this forever. I kissed her forehead and I left for the evening.

I quickly got dressed and went upstairs to help unload the groceries and put them away. My parents were in good spirits and I took their lead. Trying to enjoy what my heart yearned for but what the addict in me tried to fight. It seemed like an ongoing combat between the devil and angel at my shoulders. Hearing them argue about what to do next as if I didn't exist. Usually the angel lost but I was determined today to stay away from using longer than three days. I went to the bathroom to say a quick prayer to give me strength. I was just too tired to do this by myself. To heck with the arguments in my head I was going to pray to the Man upstairs. It's what I know, thanks to my parents.

My parents were glad to see me still home. They didn't say anything about the last two nights. Even if it was for a moment of happiness I wanted to prolong it for the sake of making them happy. And to not get into anymore fights. I think they know better than to piss me off anymore so I don't make an excuse to leave.

As it turned out, putting the food away got me hungry. I hadn't eaten in two days. The roof of my mouth was so raw and dry from smoking that I didn't think I could put food in my mouth without it hurting. I made some hot tea to help relieve my mouth and stomach so I can consume food. Mom was making one of my favorites for dinner, Arroz Caldo, a Filipino dish made with chicken and rice. I know when my mom cooks me one of my favorites it's to keep me from leaving and to make sure I eat. It was a good plan because I ate about three bowls and stayed home. It felt good.

Chapter 2

I lasted about four days before I got stir crazy, as I thought. I called Rocky and he was already partying. That was my cue to leave. The dope was already there and I didn't have to wait for it. I couldn't get there quick enough and I was jonesing even harder knowing Rocky was getting high. But I had to wait for the kids to go to sleep and my parents to turn in. As if it made any difference I could leave if I wanted to but I chose not to get in any conflict. When all was quiet, I checked in on Cord but he was still awake. I told him I was leaving and all he said was, "Whatever."

I made it to the bus on time cutting down on a walk of thirty minutes to Rocky's spot. Once I got off the bus I ran down the big hill to his place. My adrenaline was pumping fast and all I could think of was taking a big fat hit. When Rocky opened his door, I got his big bear hug. "How you doing sweetie?"

"I'm doing better now that I'm here. I thought I would go crazy sitting at home for another day."

Just then I heard other voices and it was unlike Rocky to have other people over. He likes to keep it low key as do I. The worse thing I hated was drawing attention to what we are doing. That's why I enjoyed getting high at Rocky's because it was quiet and not a lot going on but us. As I walked in and saw who was all there I knew I wasn't going to be comfortable. I can't stand these women sitting up in here. They are always sizing me up and comparing me, to what, I don't know. Besides, I wouldn't want to be like them. They don't respect themselves the way I do myself. Those who know me know I don't resort to sexual favors for drugs and they best never ask either. Heck I was called "sweet little innocent Christina" in high school, I haven't changed much since then. I may use but I always have the money to get my own. I work, so thank God I can support my own habit.

At least, not like before. I used to steal during my marriage with Russ, from big department stores until I got caught. It's what they call boosting and Russ and I, made out like bandits. Drug dealers would trade easily for anything they can get. We usually took orders, like a grocery list of things they wanted and we would go out and steal them. The time I stole from Penny's is something I will never forget about. Russ and our boys were waiting for me out in the parking lot and as soon as I got out the door I was nabbed. Just when I was being whisked away, Russ drove by me and the last thing I saw was my boys twisted around in their seats looking out the back window watching me get arrested. With another prayer and promise to God that I would never do this again, I was let go without being arrested because the items I stole was less than $200. It was two dollars short of being a felon.

Stealing was the only way we could afford our habit at times. The money I made working as a waitress and what I got from welfare was for the boys and rent. It had to, or we would be out on the streets. I always paid rent and got food for the boys before I came home with any extra money. If I didn't, Russ would convince me to spend all my money on dope instead of our bills. One time Russ got a front from a dealer without me knowing and expected me to have the money when I got home. Well, I didn't and we got into a fight, one of our biggest fights and I knew his addiction was getting worse. Funny thing was, he didn't even save any for me, he did it all himself so I was actually glad I didn't have the money. I didn't do any of it.

Right now, these girls up in here were going to do something stupid I could feel it. I think Rocky sensed it too and the air got thick. After some small talk and no interest of what they were saying, they took the hint. Within ten minutes they were on their way out. Those girls hate me and I really don't care. I don't play games, don't lie or cheat out on people and for that these girls can't stand me. Because no matter what I still have a little dignity left in me despite my using.

As soon as they left I still wasn't at ease. I had built in radar, a keen sense and one would call me paranoid but I wasn't even high yet. I was fresh. I've been right a few times so I could trust my own instincts. It's managed to get me out of trouble before anything happened while I was present. The first time I tagged someone as a narc I was right.

I tried to warn Gene, who was a drug dealer and at first wasn't quite sure about my suspicions but no sooner did I warn him that a week later Gene got busted. As long as that new guy was hanging around I never wanted to be at Gene's apartment. It's crazy how I can pick up the street wise sense and have a good judge of character. I guess that's one thing I can thank about being out in the mix. I learned I was smart, or I was just plain lucky and God was always looking out for me and gave me the insight so I can remain safe. As the night went on there were very few phone calls and no traffic in and out. I felt safer without anybody around and getting high was all I was focused on.

Chapter 3

With just a little over an hour sleep I got up quickly to get Cord and Cayden off to school. I don't like that they changed boundaries for the school district. Cord has to take the metro bus to his school out by the airport. The airport strip isn't a good place to be. I should know since my ex-boyfriend Devon and I used to deal drugs out of a motel on SeaTac strip. That game was sad and dangerous. But to be honest, it was a separate high all its own. "Cord, you're going to be late!" as I scrambled to gather all his stuff into his back pack.

"Did you see D leave yet?" asked Cord.

"No, I didn't see if he did, does it matter? Just get going cause I can't take you." D is Cord's best friend from next door and a much better friend than J.B. J.B was following in his parent's footsteps, parents that Russ and I used to get high with so I know his character. Cord ran up the stairs and he was wearing this big orange coat.

"Why are you wearing such a big heavy coat for? It's not cold out and it doesn't even fit you."

No reason, just wearing it," exclaimed Cord in his defense.

"Fine, get going and don't miss the bus coming home, I'll be at work." I can tell something was up with Cord. He didn't look at me when he answered, which led me to believe he was lying about wearing that coat. I just want him to be safe.

Papa came out of his room surprised to see me up. "Where's Isabelle?" he asked.

"She's still sleeping and I'm still tired. I'm going to lay back down for a little bit longer before I go to work. Can you get her when you hear her wake up?" No real answer, just a grunt came out of papa. Good enough for me.

Papa grabbed the coffee pot to pour water into it, "What time you go to work?"

"Eleven o'clock. I get off at six and yes I will be home." I knew he would ask me so I completed his thought for him.

"You better because I have a tennis game and your mama is going to play mahjong." Damn it, it's Friday night and I need to get a sack to make extra money. My paycheck was only going to be a couple hundred, that wasn't going to cut it for what I wanted to do. I promised Cord I'd go shopping for more school clothes.

Chapter 4

When I arrived home from work papa was on his way out to go play tennis. Isabelle, sitting in her highchair again was grinning at me with food all around her. She was happy with her food, thank goodness she was fed.

"Cord is at D's house, he come home late. You better keep an eye on him he is going to be trouble if you don't get a hold of things Christina. You need to shape up too!" Papa wasn't very happy but he left and I had to contend with the kids, as well it should be. I would just have to do business over the phone and out of the house for now till my dad got back from tennis.

"How are you babushka?" A pet name I gave Isabelle . She wiggled in her chair and gave me a motion to kiss her on her cheek. She was so smart. Adorable. I cleaned her up gave her a quick wipe down with a wash cloth and started playing with her on the living room floor. I don't do this often enough. I'm in such turmoil with my life and as much as I want to change I just don't know how to start. I've been living this life since I was 21 years old and I'm 34 years old now. God how I long to just stop. Isabelle will be 2 years old in a couple of months and Cord's already 12. Time is going by fast and I need to get a hold of my life.

"Mom?" Cord slamming through the door, "I'm going to the mall with J.B!" he announced.

"What? I thought you were with D. Come here." Leaning over the stair well looking at me I noticed he still had that big coat on. "Where did you go after school?" I asked.

"We stuck around after school and caught the next bus." Acting nonchalant.

"I thought I told you to come straight home, you know how papa is. Don't give him a heart attack worrying about your butt." He came up to me now and was just standing there with a blank look on his face. He's up to something. "Why do you have to go to the mall? You don't have any money. I told you we'll go shopping when I'm ready to. We will go on Sunday after church. You stay home." He was getting antsy and I realized at that moment what he had plans to do.

"Cord, if you are thinking about what I think you are going to do at the mall you best change your mind or I will kick your ass. That' why you have that big coat on for don't you? Don't lie to me Cord, I mean it." He didn't answer me and for the life of me was thankful that he listens to reason and knows when I mean business. I'm no fool and he knows I'm no fool. I've been around the block a few times and what he was doing was written all over him. "You tell J.B. you're not going anywhere with him anytime or anywhere. He's up to no good and to hell if you get caught up in the same shit that your dad and I did. Stealing is wrong Cord. You know what happened to me, don't do it." My mind was racing and I knew that if I don't do something to change my ways and quick, I was going to lose my son to a lifestyle that would forever change my world. It wouldn't just be me I had to keep off the streets I would have to fight for my son's as well.

Cord ran down to the basement without another word because he knew he got found out and couldn't lie to me. At the same time I think he was grateful that I was keen to his plan or else he had to go along with the gang of hoods he was hanging out with to steal. I know Cord's a good kid and subconsciously I know he doesn't want to be anything like his dad. I scooped up Isabelle and took her to my room while I changed out of my work clothes. Cord was watching TV as usual on the couch.

Chapter 5

I made a few phone calls to my connections and I had to meet up with them before my dad came home but time was running short. I hate waiting and wasting time. I had to convince my dealer to come to the house because I couldn't leave at the moment and my dad was going to be home in an hour. I have to make a transaction before that happens. Pacing the floor and peeking out the window forty five minutes later I saw headlights coming down our street. I hope that's Rico and not my dad. I went out onto the porch as if I went out to have a cigarette so Cord doesn't come out. As soon as I realized it was Rico I ran down the drive and met with him. Handed him money and got my sack. He had to make a u-turn in our dead end street and in doing so came head to head with my dad coming in. Crap that was close.

Once in my room I began to cut up the pieces of crack from the rock I spent sixty dollars on. Rico does me well and I was able to cut up at least fifteen stones, that's $300. If I wanted to and most likely will, be able to do at least three stones for myself. That's how you make profit and still get high for free, essentially anyway. Some people can't manage and end up smoking all their dope before they sell it. Me, I make sure I have people waiting on it so I don't keep it too long or I will smoke it. "Cord, come here!" He came waddling in to my room. "Here, this is how many I stones I have. This should be about $200 worth right here and this is about $100 worth." Pointing to the other pile. "Hold these till I get back with the rest of the money, when I do I will give you the fifty dollars I owe you. Okay?" He was fiddling with the stones as if to examine them.

"You make that much? How much did you buy it for?" Curious cat, but he's a smart one.

"Would you believe sixty bucks? That's why I do this. You want clothes on Sunday don't you?"

"Yeah, fine. Don't smoke any mom or I won't get my clothes, I know it." So much for caring if I smoked or not, he would rather have the clothes. He doesn't express himself very well when it comes to his concern for me but I know he does and I understood what he meant to say.

My van was working finally so I called Billy to help me make some stops. Most times I'd go alone but tonight I needed company to keep me on the straight and narrow. Billy doesn't smoke and he can help keep me in line without crossing his boundaries with me. He's my side-kick now. He was once faithful to my ex-boyfriend, Devon, but the trust never seemed to last with those two. Billy owed Devon a great deal for getting him out of a situation and keeping him safe from another dealer. We took Billy under our wing, gave him shelter, food and trust. Billy came to me one time telling me of his disappointment that Devon wouldn't trust him slinging his dope and if maybe I would trust him instead. Of course I wouldn't go against Devon even though the dope was mine and told Billy no, not this time. When Devon and I split up, that's when Billy sided with me instead.

Devon wasn't too crazy about me slinging dope on my own either, but he had no say in it. We were broke up. He decided he would rather have a life with a bunch of girls that turned tricks for us rather than to be with just me. He always professed that I was all he needed and wanted but when you have more than three girls doing everything they are told to do you're going to feel a lot of power. Men like that I'm sure. Things ended for me after the second time I caught him in the motel room with the girls. Whether anything actually happened was beside the point. The first time I caught him I kicked the door open and fought for my man. The second time it happened, I was the one that got kicked, right in the middle of my chest. That's when I knew I had to walk away. When this happened I realized that like my ex husband, drugs affected otherwise good people like Devon to do things that they would not normally do. My ex husband

and Devon were both great guys, but the drugs turned them into something unimaginable. Which I don't blame them personally, I blame the drugs.

Devon and I first met in rehab in 1994 and we hit it off real fast but we were both married at the time and we didn't explore anything further. We remained in touch here and there and after quite some time we found ourselves both divorced. We reunited in 1998 and lived together for seven months.

I was clean when we got together and Devon was struggling with his sobriety. So I helped him in his battle to stay clean. He did real well for a time and I'm sure us being together gave him a kindle of hope. Three months prior, I had given birth to my daughter Isabelle. With all three of my kids living with me and alone in our apartment Devon was a great addition. We had the best time getting to know each other and we did things with Devon that we never did with the boy's father. Devon felt the same as he never did those things with his own boys when they were young. I felt a real connection with Devon and he with me. We really and truly felt that life would be so grand if we could become a family. He definitely loved my kids and the boys were in awe of him. Devon, once a budding professional baseball player till he got injured, also became a victim to the same cruel world of drugs. He held on to the fact that I was clean and he didn't do anything to jeopardize that. He had respect for me and I appreciated it. Unlike my ex-husband who knew I was clean but always managed to lure me back into drugs because of my own weakness.

My getting back into drugs wasn't of Devon's doing but was blamed on his friend whom Devon called his brother, his best friend. Devon wasn't even around when I took that first hit. Actually Devon got mad when he heard I relapsed, which was refreshing to know that he did. But as it turned out, it opened the door for us to use together, thus Devon's fight to stay clean ended when my sobriety defunct. It had been fifteen months of clean time before I relapsed and that's what started the down whirl of my life once again.

Every time I relapsed my status picked up right where I left off as if I never quit. It would intensify with vigor and it was always harder to recover. This time around I became what I thought I would never do.

Become the drug dealer. I learned from the streets that the only way to stay on top of things and not have anyone take advantage of you is to become the one they needed and have what they wanted, your drugs and your service. Not to mention a little something, something for yourself if you're a user like I was.

Chapter 6

The decision to deal was quite simple. In order to get what I wanted and that was money for my kids' school supplies and clothes, I had to hustle drugs. Working wasn't an option because I didn't like to be restricted in a time schedule where working wouldn't allow me to do drugs. Working my own hours was more like it. And I used when I could. I also had a part time job as a cover. The first night that I started dealing, I got a twenty sack with four stones by doing a haircut. I turned the stones and by the end of the night I made $460. I never imagined it could be this easy. But when Devon and I were doing it and he had control, I never understood why we kept losing out and always spent more money. Actually, my money I got from my tax return. We spent over 4 G's in less than a month. That included living in motel rooms with our posse of tricksters and runners. Not to mention my son and daughter were with me in another room aside from our party room. Careless I know, but it was also a waste of my time and money.

I was going to be able to sell quite a bit tonight. A few stops and the last stop at Rocky's so I can enjoy some for myself. Besides, Rocky had claim on most of it and I think he has others there to buy so I should be able to go home and get the rest of my dope. Business was like clockwork and before I knew it, I had been gone two days.

I knew I was headed for a big stink whenever I did get home. Damn it, I didn't have the money for shopping for Cord. I hate it when I do this. I have $60 in my pocket. I didn't come away with what I wanted especially as busy as I was. Did a little too much smoking this time and not enough to make back. I guess this is what happened when Devon was in control of the dope. Never coming out ahead, just smoking and partying. Fortunately I gave Cord his fifty dollars when I picked up the other sack.

I ended up at Thriftway's parking lot sitting in my van trying to decide what to do with the last bit of my money. Should I buy groceries or get another sack? The answer was obvious but I was still fighting with myself. I was tired, God knows I wanted to go home but was too scared to face my parents. To see the disappointment in their faces and the disrespect I was to gain from my sons. Gosh I missed my babies. I had to think of something and think fast. Just then I looked up and I saw Pastor Jimmie sitting in a chair in front of the store. What an odd place to be sitting! He was just rocking back and forth looking out in a daze. I sensed something was wrong, yet I also knew that this was another given feed from a prayer within. I got out and as I walked towards him I became aware of an urgency to speak with him.

So I stopped right in front of him, "Hi Jimmie! What are you doing sitting here?"

He stopped rocking and looked straight at me and said, "I'm confused."

I thought that was out of context for him since he is one of the Pastors at the church I go to. "Well, come walk with me while I go shopping, we can talk." My whole demeanor changed and for the moment I felt like I was the one helping him instead of the other way around. As it turned out he was dealing with some issues with his wife. I didn't quite understand all that was going on but I tried to stay focused on what he was saying. At the same time I needed to talk to him about what I had just gone through in the past three days. My guilt and fear was getting the best of me. It always does when I come down off crack.

I paid for the groceries and Jimmie walked me to my van and loaded the bags in. I then looked at him and I said, "Jimmie, I've fucked up. I've been gone on a three day binge and I don't know how to deal with the consequences when I get home."

"Oh Chris, I'm sorry, I've been going on and on about stuff and I should have asked you how you are doing. Tell you what, lets pray right here. Do you have your bible?"

"As a matter of fact I do its right here." I crawled in the back of the van and grabbed it. He held it in one hand with mine on top of his and his other hand was on top of my head. He began to pray and I uttered with him for forgiveness. I was listening intently on what he was praying when all of a sudden his voice became more intense, the clouds starting rumbling and turning dark. He was speaking louder now telling me that he just came across a prophetic word and that it revealed to him that there will be a day sometime in August where people from all over the country will come to gather around just to see me, to listen to me, to hear what I have to offer. Just then the sky crackled and the down pour of rain hit my face and a bolt of electricity shot through my body like I've never felt before and I felt weak at the knees and buckled. Jimmie held me from a fall and I started crying. I wasn't quite sure what just happened but it seemed like something out of a movie. I know that what I presently felt was not of a normal sensation.

"Are you okay?" I nodded and was still in shock. It was raining hard and he took me in his arms and held me. "Don't worry, it's a good thing. Chris, you are meant to do far greater than you could ever imagine. I saw people surrounding you like you had something they wanted, something they needed and you had it to give. Go home, face what you have to face. God will be with you to guide you every step of the way. So you have to keep your eyes and heart open. Listen to it and it will come easily. Trust Him."

"Okay Jimmie. I'm fine now." He gave me one last squeeze and I got in the van. I sat for at least another ten minutes with tingles up my spine.

The rain stopped but the tears were still streaming down my face. I believed what happened just now, yet I question it. Why me? What do I have to offer? What can I possibly offer people? I'm a drug addict, a worthless mother and I hate myself. No one would listen to anything I have to say. Not now, not ever. "God what do you want me to do?"

Chapter 7

After that day I wasn't ever the same again. I knew in the past that I always knew God was with me even when I was getting high. Things would happen to me that was unexplainable. Nonetheless, there was only one way it could ever be possible. He had to have sent me Angels or that He had his own hand in things. The most profound thing that ever happened to me was on Easter Sunday 1997.

I was meeting up with my current boyfriend Brian for the evening and although my car wasn't working properly I had to go see him. On my way to his place my car started acting up again by fogging up the inside of my car windows so I couldn't see out. It was overheating again. I parked the car less than a quarter mile away from Brian's apartment to give it a rest then start it up again. But my time was short, it was already almost 10:00 pm and I had to be home at my parents by 11:00. I sat in my car contemplating whether to make a mad dash to his house or let the car cool down.

As I was sitting there I finally noticed a lady across the street in a white pickup truck looking straight at me. I thought it very odd of her to be on this street at this time of night just sitting there. But I paid no mind to it. She finally rolled her window down and asked if I needed help or possibly a ride. With a slight hesitation and a quick glance at my watch, straight up 10:00, I decided what harm could she pose? I said yes and locked up the car and jumped into her truck.

"Thank you so much for doing this." I said.

"No problem, all I need is for you to direct me to the freeway, I don't know where I put my map and I've been lost for some time." Wow, she was really off and how she got to this street was beyond me.

As I finally took a closer look at her I noticed she was about her mid-forty's to fifty's and she was dressed all in white, with shoulder length dirty blonde hair and porcelain like face. Harmless I thought. I pointed down the street to where Brian lived and we drove in silence. Pulling up to the apartment complex I grabbed my things and thanked her. "You have to turn around and go down this way," pointing down 1st Avenue. "You should hit the signs saying I-5 or I-90 and it will take you right where you need to go, thank you again."

As I was closing the door, she looked at me funny and said, "By the way, my name is Jolene and thank you. Take care." I slammed the door shut and ran up to Brian's apartment. Excited that I had time to spend with Brian I soon forgot about Jolene and my broken down car.

A little over an hour had passed and I was going to be late but at least I had an excuse this time. Brian had to drive me back to my car so he could look at it and or just take me home. As we were getting closer to my car Brian slowed down but didn't stop and then said "Uh, Chris, don't look at your car right now, I'll take you home and pick you up in the morning. I think your car was on fire." Oh my gosh, is that why we heard all those sirens earlier? The fire truck was for my vehicle? I couldn't believe it. I was in shock, then Brian said something even more shocking, "I'm glad you weren't in it."

When I arrived home I called the fire department to find out of any car fires and which department put it out. When I reached the right department I called them and asked what had happened to my car. They said they received a 911 call at 10:05 pm about an explosion coming from a car parked on the street. There were two loud explosions and then the car was engulfed in flames as high as 200 feet in the air. It took the firemen forty five minutes to put it out. The voice over the phone said the explosion was due to a spontaneous combustion.

The last thing the fireman said was, "You're a very lucky young lady you weren't in that car." I hung up the phone realizing just one thing. Jolene saved my life. Later, I found out that our daughter Isabelle was conceived on that very night, Easter Sunday. If Jolene wasn't there to help me, I would have died and Isabelle would not have ever been born.

Chapter 8

The near death experience was an eye opener and with the help of Brian being in my life I definitely wanted to be clean. I was feeling loved or at least treated kindly from Brian and he made me feel welcome in his family. I wanted our relationship to work. He was the first guy I dated that I didn't have any reservations with and I let myself go. The ironic thing was Brian wasn't the type of guy to be flamboyant with. Contrary to what I thought he wanted, which was not just a lay, but somebody to love and respect and call his lady. I lost his respect quicker than I ever had with any guy just because I didn't save myself long enough to know him first. I've always been quite standoffish when it came to men and what Brian saw in me was somebody totally different from who I really was.

As the tables turned on me my frustrations pent into wanting to use again, but I knew I couldn't. I had to change the sequence of abuse. When I found out I was pregnant it was another chance to redeem myself as a worthy mother. This was finally the motivation strong enough for me to quit using. It was for my unborn child and for my boys. Losing my kids was not an option. Little did I know, my daughter was an answered prayer, a gift, she definitely was a Godsend. Brian had never had the pleasure of meeting his daughter, he left me a week before Isabelle was born. Brian went back home to Pueblo, Colorado to marry the girl he left behind. I stayed clean throughout my pregnancy with Isabelle, I was proud of that.

However, no matter what good graces come my way, no matter how many times I get slapped in the face with getting a clue about my life, I revert back into my old ways. I was putting myself in danger every time I dabbled with crack, dealers and users. Consequently, I had an incident with a six inch barrel pointed at my head while I was forced to perform oral sex, right behind the alley of our apartment in Tukwila. That should have been the biggest clue to get straight. But it wasn't. My addiction was too strong.

It took me two years before I even told my husband about that incident. I couldn't tell anyone because it happened the night before I went to rehab and my husband was once again in jail. The only one that knew was our friend Eric. Mountain man, he didn't dare tell my husband because it was his weed that I was trading for when this incident happened. Eric never forgave himself and he left me alone from then on. Again, I was lucky to survive that. I thought I was dead for sure.

Chapter 9

Months had gone by since I saw Pastor Jimmy and for awhile I stopped doing dope because of what I witnessed and felt that day in the parking lot. I started going back to church and the Christmas season was coming soon. Christmas is my favorite time of the year. It's the greatest emotional high because of all the joyous memories I had as a child. A lot of my relatives would gather at our house. We had the best time opening up presents, eating all the great food and running around with my cousins that we would be sweating through our clothes. I didn't have a care in the world, just as long as we had presents, food and love, I was good to go.

My brothers and sisters and I were all good kids. We got along and we didn't give our parents any real grief. We took care of one another and we did our parents proud. In my junior year of high school I remember feeling the loneliest. My brother Tony enlisted in the Army and went to Germany. My sister Rose got married and moved to California. My other brother Denny moved down to California as well and my sister Ruth went away to college in Bellingham. It was odd being the only child. I was always looked after and sheltered by my siblings and in a short time I was all alone. It was hard at first, but I dealt with life the way my parents raised us children. To be confident, independent, strong and smart. I've quoted myself to be "my father's daughter." I believe my dad taught me more things than my other brothers and sisters since I was the only one he stayed home with as a child. He worked nights and my mom worked during the day, leaving my dad to care for me while my brothers and sisters were in school.

We are a traditional Filipino Catholic family that migrated from the Philippines in June of 1968 to Seattle. I was only three and half years old. My oldest brother Tony was twelve, Rose was eleven, Denny was ten and my closest sister was Ruth at five years old. Needless to say, my parents were old country and they didn't recognize the world of drugs and street life. They were oblivious. I remember the day my mom found out that she was watering a pot plant in my brother's room. She yanked it out as soon as she learned of it.

The only thing my family knew what to do with me was to pray since rehab didn't work. I am hoping their prayers will be answered along with my own. So far the prayers have only kept me safe and for that I am grateful.

Chapter 10

I had to try to stay clean so I could get my kids Christmas presents. This was the time of year I had to redeem myself for the things I've done wrong. I also carried the guilt I had when my ex-husband and I traded back all the boy's presents for drugs. A day in my life I will never forget and harder to ask for forgiveness. I ended up waiting in line in five below temperatures at the Salvation Army to get free presents for the boys to make up for it. More so, I know my parents were in denial the day they found out that it was my ex-husband and I that did the burglarizing of their home one Christmas Eve. Even when they established who the culprits were, they didn't kick us out of the house. I don't know how they couldn't have but I know they loved me and the boys too much to ever have us out of their eye sight. It would have been much worse than losing everything they owned.

I hate my job. Working in this shop was boring. It's slow today and the girls don't talk very good English. I wasn't making any money and sitting around was getting me edgy. I need to break away. I feel I'm sabotaging myself again. This self talk gets me in trouble and all it needs is a thought, a seed planted in my weak brain and I know I will be setting myself up for a fall. I had to make a call, but first I had to make enough tips so I can get me a sack. That or just call Rocky if he wanted to go in on one. I know he would. Just then I got a customer and I had the attention span of a seven year old racing through an inferno so I could be finished with the haircut. As quickly as I placed the clippers through the ladies hair I saw her eyes widen with a screech of a voice saying "What the hell did you do?" she exclaimed.

"You told me to cut it down really short. I even double checked to make sure that was what I understood."

"Yes I did but not that short! Oh god, just finish it already and get me the hell out of here." Well, I managed to make her feel better at the end of the cut but it made me more anxious to leave but at the rate of customers coming in and out it was going to take me forever to make any tips. So I dared to do the unthinkable. I pocketed the customers' fifty dollar bill. After I had done it, I instantly felt mortified but I couldn't undo it. The cash register could only be opened during a transaction. After work, it was a start of another binge.

Chapter 11

I ended up at the Virgil apartments down the street from my parent's house. This is the third night I had been gone and I'm so drained but for some reason I didn't feel like going home this time. I was depressed. I just wanted to keep using and numb out the feelings of loss. The life that I thought I should have had is all gone and can no longer be attained. My heart is so heavy from being broken up so many times that I couldn't bear life alone anymore. It's been over a year since Devon and I had broken up but it was still tearing me apart. I tried going back to school and I lasted a semester, I even stopped using while going to school. But again it didn't last. My college was on Pacific Highway/ SeaTac strip and there was no getting around the memories and it tempted me every day to use. I finally gave into it.

I was sitting in an easy chair of an empty apartment thinking about Devon when I heard Steve come in and said, "Devon's here looking for you."

"What! You're kidding me!" Just then Devon and his son Ricky came through the doors and I pretended to be asleep on the chair.

"Chris, what are you doing here? Your dad's been looking for you all over town. Called my mom's house worried sick about you." He was bent down next to me with much concern. Oh God I didn't want him to see me this way. Strung out and lifeless.

"I'm fine, I'm going home when I'm ready." I said.

"No, you're going home now, I told your dad I'd find you and bring you home, come on." He insisted.

I got up reluctantly because I really didn't want to go home. I looked like shit and besides, I wasn't ready to. I still wanted to get high, but with no money and dope I guess it was redundant so I went with him. We drove in silence not knowing what to say. But by the time we got to my parents street I said, "I don't want to go home Devon, stop the car."

"No Chris, are you crazy? Your kids are worried and so are your parents. I promised your dad I'd bring you home." His voice was firm and I knew I couldn't convince him so when he slowed down to my parents driveway I opened the car door and he screeched to a halt and I bolted down the street. He came after me and I should have known that he would catch up to me, he in his 6' 4" frame took fewer steps than my short 4' 10" stature. He swooped me up like a rag doll over his shoulders and headed back to my parent house. I was demanding he put me down but he didn't. Like I can make him. Ricky was standing outside the car and didn't say a word.

He got me to the front door and rang the doorbell, set me down while I held back the tears. My dad opened the door and Devon said, "There, I got her back home safe and sound like I said I would."

"I appreciate it, thank you," said my dad.

I flopped down onto the bottom stair and I started crying. Devon kneeled down and looked me straight in the eyes, "Stay home, and don't go anywhere," he said.

I put my arms around his neck and clung onto him, "Don't leave me, I helped you when you were trying to stay clean it's your turn to help me. This isn't fair, I helped you and I need you, now you're leaving me to fend for myself! I can't believe you are doing this!" I cried. He hugged me then untangled my arms and stood up.

"I got to go babe, stay home okay?" As if it was a demand and not a question. And he was gone. I ran downstairs to my room and I cried myself to sleep thinking when was I ever going to find someone to care enough about me the way I do them. I did everything for the men I loved in my life yet I never got it in return. I felt unworthy of anyone's love.

Chapter 12

I didn't slow down like I knew I should have just to spite life. Devon didn't care why should I? About me, my kids, my life. I continued to hustle and use and I was getting more calls all through the night. When I went back down to the Virgil Apartments to deliver goods, the aura was unusual. People responded to me differently, perhaps because of the other night when Devon came looking for me.

All eyes looked my way and the same Cambodian girls that I got into a fight once turned the other cheek. I sneered at them as I recalled our last encounter. I was high that night but I was walking to and from apartments selling dope and I knew they were territorial. They didn't know me because I didn't live there so they had every right to feel that way.

When I walked down the steps the Cambodian girls jumped out blocking my way and chest butted me. "What the hell," I said. The girl, who didn't look more than fifteen years old said something to her friend in Cambodian and then before I knew it they started swinging at me. I blocked her punch and hit her in the stomach and pushed her off of me. Just then guys from the 2nd floor came running down and broke us up holding my arms back. "Get off me damn it!" and boom I got hit right in the eye. The other dude didn't have a good hold of the Cambodian chick. I started kicking and the guy let me go and I shoved her so hard against the stairwell her head whiplashed. This time the guys held us apart and I was cussing at the one guy for holding me back. Called him every name in the book and told him to never fucking hold anybody's arms leaving me defenseless and giving them an open shot. Asshole.

When I got home that night it was dark but early enough that my boys were still awake. They were waiting for me and as I got in the house my younger son, Cayden started yelling at me. "Where've you been huh? You were out doing drugs again huh!! You're stupid mom!" Oh wow, that was the first time he ever spoke up like that to me about the things I do out of the house.

I looked at Cord and I knew he must have said something to his brother. Cord didn't say a word, and then he noticed my eye. "What happened to your eye mom?"

"I got into a fight." I turned away as if it was no big deal. "Some dudes held me back and the other girl had a free shot at me. If they hadn't done that I would have kicked her butt!" I exclaimed. I went to the bathroom and sure enough, my eye was black and blue. Hell that was a good shot. Damn. I got some ice and I flopped down on the couch.

Cayden came up to me angry but concerned and gave me a hug. Hopefully I don't get into another fight like that one. Thanks to Devon, I don't think it will ever happen again. The Cambodian girls left me alone this time and I continued to be more reckless and stupid in the weeks to come.

Chapter 13

My boy's lives were being destroyed, as I was falling in the cracks of motherhood. I soon realized I needed help with the boys and I called on the boys' dad to take one of them to live with him. The last time I asked Russ for help was when I was pregnant with Isabelle. But he returned both boys to me within a month even though I was seven months pregnant.

This time I was losing control and the boys were getting wilder and wilder where I couldn't get any respect or parental authority over them. I knew they were lashing out because of my absence all the time and for them not having their dad around.

My ex-husband chose to have our younger son Cayden to live with him while Cord stayed with me. The two boys have only been separated for three months once before when Russ and I attempted to make a move to Spokane, Washington. The move never worked out. No matter how hard we tried to change our lives, no matter where we moved to, the drugs always seemed to find us. As if it was a curse. After six months we moved back to Seattle.

I sent Cayden down to live with his dad in Boise and my heart was screaming. The poor boy didn't know what was actually going on but as time went on I could tell he didn't want to be living in Boise. He didn't tell me a whole lot but I can feel him. I know he missed his older brother too. I put them through a lot so I know they had to stick together in order to survive it. There were many times I had dropped them off at Angle Lake in SeaTac to let them swim or fish so I could go do drugs and deal.

In which case, they were inseparable unbeknownst to them. I made it that way. It was safer for them to be together.

The Christmas season had come and gone and without Cayden it was unbearable. I thought things would get easier but it didn't. I was a mess with or without the boys around. It was a wrong move to let Cayden go. I wanted him back. I regretted it the minute he got on that plane to his dads. A week after Christmas and only a month after Cayden left, Russ called me.

"Hey, I had to make a decision. I can't go to work and keep an eye on Cayden at the same time. I called my sister and she said she would take him in for me. But there's just one stipulation, he has to stay there for at least five years."

"WHAT! You didn't discuss this with me. Had I known you were having such a bad time why didn't you just tell me? I would have taken him back Russ! It's only been a month!"

"My sister already bought the ticket." His voice was inaudible now....

I was furious. In the back of my mind I knew very well why he couldn't have Cayden there. I was getting phone calls from his live in girlfriend almost every night about what Russ was doing. It wasn't because of his job, he was worse than I was! Not to mention the verbal abuse that never stopped with me. Oh God how could I be so stupid and do such an injustice to my children? I divorced him to give the boys a better life. Yet instead of a better life I took my boys away from one bad situation into another.

It was becoming all too clear to me now. I knew what I was doing to myself and the boys was wrong but when I saw it in a different perspective, seeing from the outside looking in to the life of Cayden and his dad, it was a familiar scene. I now know how I looked like from other people's view. I wasn't any better than Russ when it came to my obligations as a mother. The thought of it made me sick.

I cried myself to sleep again. In the morning I went to church with my parents and I think they were speechless but didn't ask questions. My parents made us kids go to church for as long as I can remember. It was because of my parents that I even still have a connection with God.

"Cord and I are going to drive down to Boise before Cayden leaves for Ohio. I have to see him one last time."

"When are you going to go?" asked my mom.

"Well, he leaves in four days. I want to spend at least a couple of days with him so we will leave on Friday."

Cord hadn't said much about the whole situation but I mentioned to him the truth of it all. I'm not going to lie to him, Cord's too smart for that. Besides, the boys spent time with their dad during Christmas one year and they didn't even celebrate it. They were staying in the shop where their dad worked in Boise. Isabelle and I were in Texas enjoying a festive celebration while my boys were cold and alone in their dads work shop. So Cord knows what it's like living with their dad. Enough said.

"Cord, we will be staying in a hotel over night, Cayden will stay with us so you guys can play or whatever." Cord and Cayden are twenty five months apart and they still like to hang out together. As we were driving I can see his mind was elsewhere. When Cord was younger he asked so many questions as if to fill his brain with data. He doesn't say much anymore. He's an observer now, and he doesn't communicate his thoughts so readily.

The long drive took us into the darkness of winter and thankfully the mountain pass wasn't snowed in. When we arrived in Boise we checked in to a hotel near the truck stop on Overland. We called Russ as soon as we got in the room. It took Russ a few hours to get over to the motel, so much so that Cord and I were almost falling asleep.

I gave Cayden a big hug. "How are you baby?"

"I'm fine mommy," as he buried his head into my chest. I bent down and I looked at him with tears welling up in my eyes. "You are going to have lots of fun at Aunt Meg and Uncle Tom's house. They will take better care of you then your dad or I can. But as soon as I get back on my feet you will be coming back to live with me and it will be sooner than this five year stuff, okay?"

He is such a tough kid but he is more emotionally high strung than his older brother. One time Cayden was jumped at a community center in South Park by five kids while his older brother watched. When I heard about it and asked Cord why he didn't help his brother, he exclaimed that he and D were watching and decided not to interfere because Cayden was taking care of it himself. Apparently Cayden kicked everybody else's butt and Cord didn't need to help him.

Amazing, but this is the same little boy that tried to run away from home after an argument that we had. Not so tough then. He packed his things in his backpack and took off on his bicycle. When it started raining really hard I got concerned. The rains in Seattle were infamous and this was no exception. I got dressed warm and went looking for him. It was raining so hard I couldn't see so well but when I found him I started running to him and remember how fast my heart was beating from relief.

"Cayden! Come on, let's hurry home. You picked a fine time to run away!" I grabbed him and held him tight.

"Mom, you didn't need to come after me, I was doing fine." I didn't say a word and started jogging up the street while he peddled his bike. We got to the short cut through the apartment complex and the rain was tapering off. In the middle of the parking lot there was this big water puddle up to my knees. Cayden got off his bike and we started walking into it. I stopped in the middle of the puddle and looked at Cayden, thinking how much I loved him. Just then I smiled and pushed Cayden down into the water and started wrestling with him. We splashed and tackled each other in the mini water hole laughing our heads off.

Then I stood up and said "Cayden, I love you so much. Just because we have a fight doesn't mean we throw the towel in. We have to work things out. Talk about it not run away. Do you understand?" He nodded his head and we hugged each other some more. "And don't you ever do this again you hear me? Especially when it's raining like this!" I smiled, kissed him on the forehead and stood holding my son in the rain. He started to cry and he said sorry.

All those memories were running through my head and now I was saying goodbye to him for the second time. I couldn't stand it but in retrospect I knew it was for the best. My life is collapsing anyway and I continue to sound like a broken record, but I again swore under my breath I would do what's right for my kids.

The next morning the boys were playing together and were having so much fun running around the parking lot with the pile of snow. I stayed in the room most of the time watching television. I was reveling in the laughter when all of a sudden I heard Cord through the open door of the room screaming, "MOM!" I ran out and Cord was hopping on one foot all the way down the corridor.

"What happened?" running to him.

Cord got onto the bed and just kept saying oh my god, oh my god. He lifted up his pant leg and there I saw the skin of his leg ripped open to the bone.

"Ah shit! Damn it!" I ran to the phone and called 911. I grabbed towels and put pressure onto his leg to keep from bleeding but oddly enough it wasn't bleeding too much at all. We took him to the hospital and he ended up with fourteen stitches.

Sunday morning, we headed back to Seattle prior to Cayden leaving the next day to Ohio. I couldn't stand to see him board that plane. It was better that we left first. When Cord finally fell asleep while on the road, I had my cry and was left with my thoughts about my life, the future of my kids and where it was headed. The eight hours home gave me ample time to ponder and another opportunity to speak to God with a clear head and a heavy heart.

Chapter 14

The new millennium just past and starting it off by sending my son away was not the manner in which I wanted it to commence. I had a simple notion and that was to refrain from doing what I was doing but relentlessly I didn't know how to embark on that path. I drove around and around and ended up on Alki beach. It was still cold so I stayed in the car looking out into the waters.

I don't know how many times I've come to this point in my life. Seeking, searching and yearning for an answer. The one thing that my mom had instilled in me was to seek guidance from God. To always pray. I wanted to, especially at this moment and I had in the past. But sometimes I feel I am not worthy of HIS grace. I've asked HIM too many times for help and I constantly let Him down. But I know through the foundation of my upbringing that God is a forgiving God, so I presume I have to forgive myself first. That would be my first step. Then I can feel better about asking HIM forgiveness.

Still deep in thought I remember the first time I went to rehab. Once in 1992 and second time in 1994. The first time, my family had an intervention during my son Cord's 4th birthday party. That really sucked for them to do that during his party but I understand now why they did it. I was higher than a kite that day of my son's party. I made myself scarce by taking trips to the bathroom and getting high while the party was going on upstairs of my parents house. I now know that my family knew what I was doing the entire time. I wasn't fooling anyone. Not even my son. The thought of my son kicking the bathroom door while I was taking a hit makes me cringe. All he wanted to do was open his presents.

When all of Cords friends left, my family came together in the living room to sit down and talk to me about my habit. I loathed everyone at the time. Putting me on the spot and making me feel out of sorts, especially in front of Cord. But he didn't know any better. When I finally conceded to going to treatment my only thoughts were of my boys. I spoke to Cord and told him that mommy was sick and was going to a hospital to get better. He didn't have a clue and smiled at me and said, "Get better mommy."

There was one thing missing in that equation. My husband Russ wasn't getting any help and he needed it just as much as I did. We both experienced free basing for the first time on New Year's eve of 1986. We grew in our addiction together. My heart ached with that thought, I went back downstairs after the intervention and locked myself in my room. I didn't want to think of anything else so I finished off the rest of my crack that I had in my pocket. When I finished I cried myself to sleep for the hundredth time.

A whole month in rehab and tens of thousands of dollars later, a week after completing it, I relapsed. It wasn't easy staying clean while my husband was still using. Needless to say, it was another waste of money on me that my family had to swallow. The first time my family spent money on me was when they gave me a chance to open a beauty salon in 1986 from ground zero. Seven months later Russ and I defaulted by smoking up the money left over from the loan. Over thirty five grand in all that we had to build the salon and maybe three grand that we used on our addiction to cocaine. I remember that evening when Russ and I told my dad of our problem and the demise of the shop. My dad was in shock and didn't know the first thing about addiction the way Russ and I had it. I felt sick to my stomach. Literally, since I also found out I was three months pregnant with Cord.

I kept my relapse a secret from my family for at least six months. It was inevitable that they would find out. The second occasion of rehab was when I got caught stealing from JCPenney's and instead of going to jail I admitted myself into rehab at Cedar Hills. My family didn't know about the pending theft charge other than me wanting to get cleaned up. They couldn't take any more bad news as it was and being prosecuted was the last thing they needed to know. I separated from Russ because I knew with him still using, I wasn't going to stay clean. Russ moved to Boise. I just wished he would have cleaned up too so we could have a normal life with our boys.

Rehab was better the second time around and I think it was because I quit three weeks before going in. After rehab and once I remained clean for seven months my boy's dad encouraged us to join him in Boise. I was hopeful and so eager to start a better lifestyle for all of us and especially for the boys. Russ promised me that he was clean and I was adamant about him not using. So I trusted what he said and we moved to Boise. I just wanted ordinariness, structure and love. That's all I wanted.

For the first time in our seven years of marriage, we were normal. I loved every minute of life with Russ and the boys. We were both working, played together, ate dinner together, took drives and the boys and I prayed the rosary every Sunday. Life was finally good, exactly what I sought after.

My relationship with Russ took some getting used to. We were both clean! Russ was actually a nice guy. The same guy I remember meeting. He laughed and joked around and was really good with the boys. He did things around the house, bought the boys toys he even sent me flowers on Valentine's Day! The first time he ever did that and I was in awe. He was tickled himself to see my face when the flowers arrived at our door. It was the first genuine gesture he expressed to me in all the years that we were married. I fell in love with him all over again. It was good to see him for who he really was without the influence of drugs. I was hoping my being clean had helped him see the better life that we could have together. For the most part, it did. But nothing seemed to last. Drugs seeped back into our lives like the plague.

Four months after we moved to Boise, Russ got restless and started using again and I caught him. Long story short, I got pulled back into doing drugs once more after fighting with Russ and with myself. My addiction decided to join in instead of getting beat up emotionally over it. It had conquered my sobriety after eleven hard earned months. A year later, Russ and I got a divorce and I was left with a broken home and grief stricken kids.

Looking out the window of my car I fell envious of the couple walking their dogs and how happy they were together. I wanted so much for my marriage to work but having two addicts wasn't an ideal combination. It was the only thing that kept us together. Using was what made our relationship work. But it wasn't what I wanted. Looking back on Mother's day of that year, I don't regret what I did by asking for a divorce. It was the best thing I could have done if I wanted a life for me and the boys to exist.

It was a cycle of measures that seemed to replicate over and over again. It was the last time my husband's harsh words would ever affect me. I didn't deserve to be treated that way. The addict in him became abusive yet again and I wouldn't tolerate it. The one good thing about rehab was that I learned to defend myself and it gave me tools to live by. Being co-dependent was no longer an issue with me. The submissive, naïve, docile wife that I was no longer existed as well. People couldn't govern my emotions that I couldn't think on my own. I had the power of knowledge to strengthen me, knowing God and rehab helped with that. Being drug free gave me strength that I never knew I had. Drugs clouded my ambitions. I knew this to be true and I know I can be a better person if I could just stick to my convictions.

Chapter 15

I pulled out from my parking spot since the sun was now trouncing beyond the horizon. I roamed down the street to head back home and I made a resolution to stay clean for as long as I can so I can make that next move, whatever it was. I was confident. I was nearly home when I noticed Poppy and Leo walking on the side of the road by the crack house. Damn it, I have to get home. Sure enough they waved me down and what do I do? I stopped and they both scrambled in the van.

"Mom, so glad you're here, we need a ride. Take us to 188th we'll hook you up!" *Oh for the love of God! Can't I ever say no? I'm cursing and screaming inside can't you hear it? I want out so bad and I was just talking to you Lord why must you test my every move? I'm still weak, I need your strength I can't do this on my own anymore!*

"Guys, this better be quick because I need to get home. I told my parents I'd be back already." Not that they believed me but I wanted to make an attempt at being honest for once and stick to my word.

"Oh it will be, he's waiting on us this time, and we just have to get there before he leaves." Poppy talks so fast. She's just a kid. Sixteen I think. And her boyfriend Leo was eighteen. A scrawny little kid at that. He had spunk and charisma too. They called me mom because I got them out of a jam before, gave them money and food after they got jacked for their stuff. Never did know who beat up Leo one night. Since then we got close and I called them my kids. They found a sense of security being around me. I had an upper edge on the streets. The same way I felt when I was known for being Devon's lady. Now I didn't need that refuge from Devon. I was totally on my own.

We drove the twenty minutes to 188th at SeaTac, close to the seven eleven store, dumb place to meet up. I drove into the gas station next door to pump gas while the two kids walked over to the other store. I took my time because situations like this, never goes smoothly and I didn't want to look anxious or draw attention to myself. I walked into the gas station, got something to drink and as I was paying for my gas I can see out the corner of my eye the kids racing towards my van, opening the door, getting in and ducking. Damn it, something was up and all I knew was this looked like trouble. I got my change, said a pleasant thank you and walked quickly to the van. Without looking at the kids I started talking to them. "What the hell did you guys do? Shit never mind I don't want to know!"

"Just pull out and go, go, go Chris!" Leo said. Motherfucker. They just jacked someone I know it. I pulled out and went the opposite direction of seven eleven. We all started yelling at the same time with me swearing at them louder. I had to calm down, my anxiety was getting to me. I drove the back roads and to my surprise no one was following us. They actually got away with it.

"Is anyone following us?" Poppy asked still hiding down low.

"No, no one, but stay down anyways and tell me what happened." I was pissed.

"Dude, we got the shit but we had to get out of there before they found out the rolled up money were all ones." Leo explained.

"How much did you get and for how much?" feeling my urges peak knowing they had the dope.

"We got an ounce and only paid $150 for it!" Poppy was laughing now. Holy crap they got away with that?

"This shit's gonna get back to you, you know that right?"

"We'll sell the shit and give him the money later." Leo was sure of himself.

"Why didn't you just ask him for a front you ding bat?" I took a right down Des Moines Way.

"He wouldn't let us. We wanted to prove to him that we could do it on a front but he was being a jerk. Anyhow, we got it handled Chris, sorry

we didn't tell you first. You wouldn't have driven us if we told you first."
Damn right I wouldn't have.

"Is it cooked up or powder?" I wondered.

"Its powder, we got to go somewhere and cook it but I don't want to
go back to the hole." The hole meaning our spot, crack house down by
my parent's house where I picked them up at. I can't believe this. This
is going to be a lot longer than I needed this to take. But I wasn't going
to bail now and not get any stuff for what I did for them.

"I'm dropping you off and you guys can decide where to go, I'm not
hanging with you long enough to cook this shit up or drive any further.
So give me a damn gram and I will do it myself at home." I was adamant
about it.

"Chris, let's go to your house, this way we can just walk back down
to the hole when we are done." Poppy sat up now and was looking
around.

"Hell no, you guys put this on yourselves I don't want you near my
parents house or my kids. You hear me?" I eyed Poppy in the rear view
mirror and gave her a hard stare. "Leo, break that shit up and give me a
gram. Then I'm dropping you off." Poppy was about to say something
else, "Leo, you hear me?" I said louder.

"Yeah, yeah, I heard you." Leo answered while the baggy was in his
mouth trying to get the knot undone. While he was trying to pile the coke
in a piece of paper I circled the block a couple times and decided I would
drop them off in White Center somewhere. They knew a few people out
there they could hook up with and they would be fine. I just wanted out
of the situation and quick. I never dealt my business this way before and
I wasn't going to be a part of it now. I dropped them off and it was already
eleven twenty. Shit, the kids are probably in bed by now and if I went
home I'd get yelled at again. So I might as well stay out. I headed over to
Rocky's apartment, I know he will be awake and happy to see me.

Rocky was alone this time and that worked out to our benefit. I was
able to cook up the stuff and to my surprise the coke came back pretty
good. Rocky and I have always gotten along really well. He trusted me
and I trusted him. I'm the only one that he has allowed to do certain things
in his spot. Like answer his phone, answer his door, let him know which

people shouldn't be allowed in his place which was rare because it wasn't any of my business, but I would show my dislike for certain people and that was good enough for Rocky. I was referred to as the "Lady of the house" and I had a lot of say over some of the women that usually try to manipulate Rocky's attention, or otherwise trying to control the shit going on in his spot.

It's crazy out in the mix, these women were so competitive and men are always trying to claim stake on some bitch to do their dirty work or to just be their bitch. I wasn't anybodies bitch, I ran and did my own thing and that's what the other girls didn't like.

We hung out and smoked dope for a couple of hours till people started knocking on Rocky's door. I didn't want to stay, I was feeling out of sorts all day anyways and I just wanted to be alone. So I left. When I got home I looked in on Isabelle and stared at her while she slept. I picked her up and held her close to my heart. The fragrant of her hair was freshly washed. Mom must have given her a bath tonight. As I rocked Isabelle side to side, I closed my eyes and I began to pray for a miracle. A miracle that would wisk me and my kids away from all of this. I laid Isabelle back in her crib, "I love you baby girl, say a prayer for your mama."

Chapter 16

 My room was a mess and I started picking it up. It's past two
o'clock in the morning and I had a lot of dope left. It would take
me more than a day to finish it by myself. I made a few phone
calls to see if anybody needed any stuff but nobody answered their cell
phones. I should have stayed at Rocky's, I'm sure someone would have
bought some but I didn't want to go back over there right now.

I fell asleep only to be woken up by the alarm being turned off at the
front door. Next, the door slammed shut and I could hear my parents
leaving. Dang, I must of have needed the sleep, I slept through the night.
My dad takes my mom to work every morning and by now my son should
be on his way out to catch the bus as well.

Thank goodness Isabelle was still asleep. Well this was a good a time
as any to take a wake me up hit. Sitting up in my bed I could see my
reflection off the mirror on the closet door. I lit my pipe to melt the rock
and I got up, stood in front of that mirror and watched myself. The first
hit of the day was always the best. You end up chasing it the rest of the
day. But as I looked in the mirror, it wasn't what I expected to see. It
wasn't me or so I thought, but a blur of something unrecognizable. A
smudge of a ghost-like figure? I stepped away, put my pipe in my drawer
and took a shower before Isabelle woke up. Was that who I thought it
was?

Chapter 17

It's tax season. I went to the tax preparer who Rocky referred me to. I was told this CPA could get me a better refund than others. I get a lot of money with my EIC alone so whatever extra I can obtain would be an added plus. In the meantime I didn't have any cash of my own and I needed to save for whatever I do next to get out of this hell hole. I had to go out and hustle again for awhile. I figured with my refund and slinging dope I should have over four grand.

I managed a front from Rico and normally he does me double so I could make extra money. He does that because he knows I'm good for it and I have kids to buy things for. Not to mention I've never stiffed him and always paid him back. I always sensed that Rico was holding on to the fact that he would someday convince me to be one of his "ladies," which is why he was being so nice. I tried to act indifferent and pretended not to have a clue of his intentions so I could get away with being a little naïve. It was a game of survival, it always worked. Besides, I would be on a lot of women's shit list if I became Rico's lady. A lot of ladies wanted to be Rico's number one and the girl that was, was in jail. It wasn't my scene to be obligated to anyone but myself.

Before I met Rico I was hanging out at this one house in South Park and it was one crazy party house. The "lady" of the house, Tannya, was a bad ass and she could beat you up just as well as the next guy. She beat up her old man all the time. She was a conniving, manipulative, sinful person at which I was a victim of one of her games. Call me inexperienced, call me stupid, call me what you want but after it was all said and done I was shameful, embarrassed and from that moment on knew what it felt like to be used. I knew I was fresh to the mix and the games of the street and educating yourself had to be done by making mistakes. No one is gonna tell you what to look out for. Everyone is for themselves. There's no hand book on survival. Or should I say, the school of "Hard Knocks?"

If you didn't survive you would be turned on, beaten up, taken for or used at people's disposal. In my lowliest of times this is one of the worst moments of my being in the mix that I would never admit to but it happened. At the same time, my thoughts of that situation is what keeps me focused on what is now going on around me. A lesson learned.

Chapter 18

Tannya was good and she knew exactly what she was doing when she had asked me to take her somewhere to get some stuff. To meet up with another dealer named Tory. For the ride, I would get a kick back plus I wanted to buy forty dollars worth. In my naïve world I went along with everything and took her to meet with Tory at a motel off of East Marginal Way. A dump of a place but it was in the middle of the afternoon and I didn't feel threatened.

Tannya and Tory were conversing and debating out in the parking lot that took forever and I was getting antsy. Finally Tory opened the hood of his car and removed something from the inside of the engine. It was his stash. We all went inside the motel room and they exchanged words for a bit, Tory threw a baggy at her and she gave him a big hug and smile.

"Chris, give me your keys and wait for me, I will be right back to get you."

"Why, where you going?" I said.

"Just stay here, I'll be back. Tory's a nice guy, he won't bite. You could get to know him better." And she winked at him.

She took off and Tory and I just sat across from each other at the table and didn't say a word. I was nervous and I kept roaming my eyes all around the room. Then Tory took out a rock and handed it to me across the table. I looked at him and I had an uneasy feeling about the whole situation but wouldn't you know it, I was jonesing for a hit and my judgment was non-existent.

He took my hand, walked around the table and whispered in my ear. I hesitated for a moment, got up, went to the bathroom and stared at the reflection in the dirty plastic of a mirror. I took a hit to make myself numb and drift off in a world that wouldn't allow me to focus on what was about to happen. I didn't want to believe that Tannya set me up. She played me for a trick and now I had to be Tory's date. He paid Tannya for my services with dope. I was in complete shock. I had been telling people that I don't resort to behavior like this and now I had to become the one thing that I swore I would never do. It was bad enough I was a drug addict but I would never stoop so low as to do things like this. This will definitely get out in the mix with Tannya's big mouth. My only argument would be to tell the truth. I will never forget or forgive what Tannya did to me.

That incident changed how I began to operate in the mix. I had to pay much more attention to what was going on, what was being said and who was around me. Never trusting anyone and becoming the one thing that would keep you alive in the mix. Smarter and more devious than all the rest. I stayed away from Tannya as much as possible. The only time I visited her was to get to know who her connections were. I needed to cut her off but not before I was able to steal her main connection, Rico.

Rico was top dog and he was the one I needed to get to know. I finally had a chance to drive Lisa, Tannya's friend to hook up with Rico. Since I was just the driver I wasn't allowed in the house but when we got to his house, my luck changed. Rico was standing outside on the street and he came right to us. Rico approached my window instead of Lisa's with a curious look on his face. It was perfect. Better than what I had planned. From the moment I smiled at him, flirted just a bit and told him my name, it was history. Tannya was no longer needed.

Chapter 19

I got my fat rock that could last me a week. I like it when Rico has it all cooked up for me in one chunk. It gave me the opportunity to shave the pieces down to what I thought was a good twenty piece and kept the shavings for my personal stash. Down at the Virgil apartment's, Danny gave me a plate of shavings from the rocks he cut up and it amounted to about a gram. That's how I found out the shavings were better for me to smoke. It lasted me longer and was easier to smoke. Easier to hide too.

I went down to my old stomping grounds on Pac-Hwy, SeaTac airport strip. It's the same spots that Devon and I used to hang out at in the motels. We used to occupy two adjoining rooms, one would be the clean room and one would be the party room where we do our dealings in. I hardly ever went in the party room. There were always too many people there smoking up a storm, it made me nervous. The fact that the room was in my name was a big concern and Devon wasn't there to regulate it all the time and I was still naïve to do anything about it. I hated the feeling of not being able to speak my mind when I needed to.

There was a day that I was in the party room and people kept coming in and I couldn't control the chaos. Just then Devon walked in like the big man on campus and raised his voice to say one thing and everyone scattered. I was so thankful he did that but he looked at me as if I was the cause of it. Little did he know, those people didn't give me the time of day when I open my mouth the way that they do with him. But I respected him in the sense that he can carry his own weight around without pounding people to the ground, like other badass dealers. People listened to him and I liked that trait.

Driving down the streets gave me a chill. The memories of me and Devon were overwhelming. I decided to turn around and go to South Park instead. I stopped at the store to get some smokes, that's when I saw JJ.

"Oh my gosh! Look what the cat drug in!" I exclaimed. He swooped me up like a rag doll and gave me a hug. I couldn't remember the last time I saw him but our dating was brief and a rebound from Devon. From one drug dealer boyfriend to another drug dealer boyfriend. I should have learned from the first time.

"What are you doing here Chris? I thought you quit?" JJ raised his eyebrow.

"Yeah, well, I tried. Just like you, I thought you quit too. What are you doing here?" as I started walking back to my van.

"Nothing, just hanging around. I'm getting married next month." He was leaning over me in my van now.

"You got to be kidding? So quick? Do you even know this women very well?" I put the key in the ignition.

"No matter, I know her well enough. I know you too I'd marry you!" He was getting too close for comfort now. I started up my van.

"Well, if I were you, I'd check your loyalty before getting married to anyone, have a good life, see ya!"

He slammed my door and I started backing out of the lot. I can't believe I was his lady at one time. Not even two weeks and we broke up over something I had no idea of what it was. I didn't care. It was too much drama for me anyway. We were on the verge of competing against one another for territory. We were both dealing out of the same spots out on Sea-Tac strip, along with at least ten other low life dealers trying to sling. If you had the best dope or deals you will get the business quicker than others. Just don't dog anybody in the process. Protocol.

Chapter 20

My cell phone was ringing and I couldn't reach it. Dang it, don't want to miss a call it could be someone wanting some stuff. I pulled into a neighborhood, swerved to the curb and grabbed my phone real quick. "Hello, who's this?"

"Mom, where are you?" It wasn't my own kid, but it was Poppy.

"I'm on the road, what do you need, I'm busy." I was a bit irritated.

"Me and Leo are out of stuff, can you get any?"

"Actually, I was on my way there anyways. I'm holding right now so I'll be there in a little bit." I started driving off and the phone clicked.

There must be some money sitting there to be spent. In the mean time, I thought I would take a hit while I was driving. Normally I wouldn't when I know I needed to sell my dope but since there was people waiting I knew I would get mine anyway. I enjoyed doing it in the car, I felt safer knowing no one was around to bust me. But, I do drive slower when I'm high. I got to the house a half hour later then I said I would be.

I had to park my van where my parents couldn't see it because the crack house was just down Des Moines Memorial drive, walking distance from my parents to be exact. When I walked in after knocking, everyone was in their seats or in the kitchen.

"Hey, what's up?" Everyone bounced up out of their chairs. "Geez, you guys been waiting long or what?" I started laughing. I went straight into the back bedroom and a few peeps followed me. "Where's Poppy and Leo?" I sat on the bed.

A voice from the bathroom yelled out, "They went to the store they'll be back."

Most of these cats in here I don't even know, but I've dealt with them before. A few I knew for awhile, Ted was sitting across from me. "Did Poppy tell you I'd be here?" I asked.

"Yeah, she did. Been waiting awhile, nobody seems to be around right now, no one calling back. We didn't think you'd get here either."

"Well, I had to take a detour for a minute, but I'm here now. So what's up, what do you need?" I started digging in my pocket for my sack and pipe. "How much money you got?"

"I got fifty, will you do me good?" Ted was almost pleading.

"I do what I can which is most of the time. You haven't made any complaints before, right?" I pulled out four big stones, cut a piece out of one of them and put it in my pipe. Ted laid the money on the nightstand and I handed him the stones. He gave me a big smile and jetted out of the room practically bumping into Poppy and Leo at the doorway.

"Mom, shit couldn't you wait for us?" Leo said.

"Wait, what the fuck for?" I started heating up my pipe to take a hit. "I got enough for you, I just sold some to Teddy, that's it. There are four other peeps out there for you to deal with. You called me remember?" I took my hit and they shut up.

The night was productive and there were a lot of people coming in and out the house by ten o'clock. Getting high was becoming a hindrance, I knew I had to cut out soon. Damn shit gets me paranoid.

Chapter 21

The last time I was in this house we all thought it was going to get bammer rammed. The parking lot was blocked off by the police and we all panicked. I called my friend Justin who was, of all people, a police officer. I told him what was going on and he told me to get out of the house right away. To pick up my shit and leave.

I couldn't believe what he was telling me but I listened to him. He had me stay on the phone while I walked out and everyone in the house was yelling at me to stay put. Justin kept telling me to keep walking so I did and went right past the police line while talking to him on the phone. Damn if I thought I was going to get busted. Justin stayed on the phone while I walked up the street to my parent's house.

Once there he made me promise him to stay home for the rest of the night, and I did. I was safe. Justin's a cop but he's my friend too. He knew what I was doing and it was wrong at times to make him feel like he needed to protect me from myself. He helped me out of situations more than once. When I was on a binge he called my parents and he picked my dad up to come get me. He never judged me and always thought that I didn't belong in the mix which is why he helped me when he could without crossing the line of him being a cop. He was right about me not belonging in the mix, I just couldn't believe it at the time.

Reminiscing that day in this house made me realize I shouldn't be in one spot all night. It was dangerous. I had to re-up anyways so I made my way out of there and called Rico to come meet me again. He was happy to hear from me since I told him I'd call him in the morning, but this time

I only made enough to pay him back and re-up. This next sack the sales will be all mine. I'm looking to make at least $400 if I keep on top of things.

Chapter 22

I was set to meet with Rico in our usual location in White Center but he had me waiting so dang long that I almost had to leave. Sitting in my car for more than twenty minutes is not a very good sign. Especially late at night. My battery was going out on my cell phone and I didn't want to have to use the pay phone. I attempted to call him hoping my phone didn't cut out in the middle of it ringing.

Just as I was dialing I saw Rico approaching in one entry while in the next entrance of the lot were the police. Shit, Rico answered the phone and all he said was, "Follow me." And hung up. I waited for him to cross the medium before I started my van and head out after him slowly. So many things were running through my head. My adrenaline pumping and my nerves were getting shot. I don't know what I would do if I ever got caught. I just hoped and prayed that I wouldn't. This is the same damn reason why I need to get out of what I am doing. My kids and family would be so devastated if I had to go to jail over this stupid shit. But here I am, being stupid.

I followed Rico down Roseburg and took another right towards Rusty's house. We drove up the drive and he abruptly parked his car, walked to my window and just plowed into me.

"God damn don't be wasting my time with this tidily shit. I don't have time for it!" Wow, I've never seen him mad before. I just stared at him and in my meek voice, said "Here." And handed him his money.

"It's doubled and I need another sack. I won't be bothering you anymore tonight. I should have enough for a couple of days."

"Come on!" He said. We walked up into the trailer home and I sat down. Place was so dark and dingy. Rusty wasn't home.

"I hate those goddamn cops. I didn't mean to yell at you. You're pretty straight up, wasn't you I was yelling at." He mumbled something else but I couldn't understand him. I can tell he was smoking a lot tonight. Yeah, he was paranoid too, no wonder he took things out on me. We heard Rusty and another voice walking up the driveway and before the door opened I gave Rico another bundle of money, "There are two bills, and I'll get out of your hair."

"It's not cooked, but I'll give you extra in case you fuck it up cooking it." He smiled at me and gave me a chunk of cooked up shit and another baggy of powder. I never look at the stuff, a sign of my respect. I keep it in my fists trusting that it's what I paid for until I'm completely out of the house. I never stayed to get high with Rico, as hot as he was I didn't want to be around him any longer than I had to. Plus there's no telling what stupid ideas he would have to make things more interesting other than smoking. I didn't want that opportunity to present itself so I jetted out as soon as I got my dope. "Thanks, Rico!"

Chapter 23

On the third day of being gone, I knew I had to get a change of clothes, showered and some sleep. I left the crack house at six o'clock in the morning and got to my parent's house in time for my dad to take my mom to work. I ran downstairs and grabbed my clothes from my room and stuffed it in a bag. Just as I was doing that I heard something and I froze.

I listened closely and then I realized I was hearing crying from above me. It was my son. Was he sobbing. But why? Because of me? Did he hear me come home? Oh my God, he must be crying because of me. I slumped on my bed and stared into the damn mirror hanging on my closet door again. Oh Lord what am I doing? Must I continue with this farce of a life? It's not even a life. This isn't living! I have to get out of this and now.

The tears were flowing down my face as I listened to Cord cry. I tore a piece of paper from a binder and I began to write.

"Dear Son, I'm sorry for all the things that I am doing. I know you must hate me by now but I've made a decision and I'm going to stop all that I am doing. This is final. I promise. But I have to take care of some business first and then I will be done with it. I will be home with you and your sister. I love you Cord, don't give up on me just yet. Love, Mom."

I wiped the tears off the paper and folded it up. I got the rest of my clothes and essentials into my bag and ran upstairs. I kissed the letter and shoved it under Cords bedroom door. "I'll be back son and things will be okay." I whispered.

Chapter 24

I ran down the path through the apartments below my parent's house and waited for my dad to arrive so I wouldn't bump into him on the main street while walking. As soon as he drove up I continued on my way to the crack house. I still had welled up tears in my eyes and as soon as I got to the house I went straight to the bathroom, sat on the toilet seat and took a big fat hit.

This fucked up drug has ruined my life! But damn if I can't stop doing this. I sat there higher than a kite. God! Help Me! I jumped when I heard the knock on the bathroom door. Shit, now what. "Come!" I said.

"Hey Chris, got a hit?" It was Jeff.

"Gahd, can't I take a hit and enjoy it before you barge in here? Why? You need a hit, want a hit or are you going to buy any?" I stood up and he came in next to me facing the mirror. You look like shit Chris, looking at myself and I couldn't believe what I was looking at. Dark circles, sunken face and ratty hair.

"I got twenty bucks that's all I got and I need to go meet my ma in a little while." He picked at his face while looking at himself in the mirror.

"Dude, if you are going to see your mom, you are not going to be all fucked up like you are." For some reason I'm always looking out for these assholes and I don't know what compels me to do that. "Look, I'll give you a hit but don't ask me for nothing else because you need to go on. Go eat with that money man. Here." I gave Jeff a bump. "I have to take a shower okay?"

He walked out and I locked the door behind him. When I turned around, I was face to face with myself in that mirror. I took another toke off my pipe while watching. Then I started to cry all over again. I started the shower so no one would hear me. I wrapped all my shit together and put it in a pile far from the bathroom door where I can see it. No matter what, I don't ever trust these guys in here, even if I am in the shower and the doors locked. These cats are sly.

I got in the shower and my sobs became deeper and I began pulling my hair in desperation. My son, my kids, I cried with my heart breaking with every drop of tear. I got out from under the spray of water and leaned my back against the tiled wall, that's when I heard Him. I put my hands to my face to wipe off the water. I looked up as if to hear better but there was nothing, so I thought. What did I hear? I picked up the bottle of shampoo and started washing my hair.

"You have to leave." Oh my God, who was that? I quickly rinsed the shampoo out of my hair and off my eyes.

"What?" I said, and peeked out the shower curtain. No one was there. Oh God I'm going crazy hearing things. I know I haven't had any sleep but I'm not that messed up. I know factual from fiction!

"You have to leave Seattle." There it was again! It was definitely a voice. Not inside my head, not my imagination. I wiped my eyes again and looked up as if I would see His face.

I said, "What? Are you kidding me? Did I hear you say I have to leave Seattle, my home?"

"Yes, my child, you heard correct." Okay, no one says my child if you weren't the Holy One. Yet I was skeptical.

"Oh yea, and where would I go?" I asked sarcastically.

"To Boise." It said. I started laughing!

"Boise? Idaho? What in the world is in Boise, Idaho?" I exclaimed. This can't be real. No way am I having a conversation like this, yet I was. But how can I be sure this is authentic? Oh Lord if only this was true, please help me.

"It is Holy Land, my land and you must go there." His voice didn't skip a beat.

"But I thought all of the land is yours, what's so different about Boise of all places?" I put conditioner in my hair as if this was a normal conversation.

"All of the lands are mine yes, but Boise is where you will find peace." His voice was loving and tender.

"But what will I do there, where will I go and do? I don't have a job or a place to live there!" I rinsed the conditioner out and started washing my body. I don't know why He would send me there. Doesn't He remember what I went through the last time I was in Boise? I was so depressed that I almost killed myself!

"If you obey me I will provide you with everything you need."

"That's it? That's all? Just go and let my faith in You lead me to whatever?"

That was a tall order to just pack up and leave without a plan. Yet I had nothing to lose really. But it was crazy! There were no grounds for me to go back to a place of despair! I have nothing there. No family, no job or friends. I had to process this but, I do need to get out of Seattle and I've needed an answer as to what to do. Is He really giving me a reply to my prayers! Maybe He is the answer? Nothing else has worked. Rehab didn't work, my families ultimatums didn't work, when I lost everything it didn't faze me. I tried hundreds of times to do it myself with no luck. Ok, fine, what the heck.

"When would I leave? How will I know when to go?" If I could get better then it was worth a try and I needed HIM because I had nothing else.

"You will know when, I will be with you all the way." Oh my God, my God, I can't believe this is happening.

All these years of pleading, begging, praying, and crying for help and now you come to me like this? In a shower of a crack house! You are amazing! Only you could pull this off! No one is ever going to believe this!

"My Lord I had every faith in YOU and I promised so many times to be good. Why are you still giving me another chance?"

"You have work to do that only you can do."

"And what would that be?"

"In due time, you will know what it is you must do."

I turned off the shower and got out. I quickly dried myself and wiped the steam from the mirrors. I looked at myself again. Are you sure you're not hearing things Christina? I asked myself and I began to laugh and you know what, I didn't care if I was hearing things but I knew I wasn't crazy. At least I had my mind focused on something more positive for a change. I got dressed, opened the bathroom door and Poppy came in. "What's up?"

"Actually, I feel pretty good, what's up with you?" I turned and looked at her.

"I need a sack, here." She tossed the money on the counter.

"I don't know if I have that much but, hang on a second okay?" I sat back on the toilet to get my shoes on. She walked out.

"No one is going to believe this." I whispered under my breath.

"Yes they will. They will listen to you." Oh my gosh, He was still there!

"No they won't, they'll all laugh at me for sure." I grabbed my makeup out of my purse and starting putting my eyes in place.

"You will be surprised." And that was the last I heard of HIM.

Okay, I know what I heard and I heard His voice tell me I had to go to Boise. I started laughing hysterically again. I heard someone yell from the living room. What the hell's so funny?' Out of habit, I lit up a hit off my pipe and if I didn't know better, I didn't feel a damn thing! I tried another toke and again I couldn't get off on it! Shit! I looked at the mirror and My God, there You were! I threw my pipe away, grabbed my stuff and ran out into the living room.

"What is up with you, Chris? Laughing all to yourself, what's up?" Shannon asked.

"I am going to Boise! Yup I'm done with this shit and I am getting out of this hell hole!" I was beaming by now.

I sat next to Jerry at the kitchen table and Shannon across from me. "Wow, really? You're leaving just like that? Man, I wish I could do that." Shannon looked at me with eyes that looked like mine an hour ago.

"But you can Shannon. You just have to get up and do it." Throwing my hands up in the air.

I guess He was right, no one was laughing at me. Not yet anyway. "You have to have faith and trust in God to help you get through all this."

There I said it. Silence. Oh my, this is creepy. Everyone was listening now. There were seven people all around me listening attentively.

"Did you know God is with you every step of the way? All He wants is for you to follow Him. He holds no grudges. All of you, you can get out of this, you can leave all of this!" I'm in shock! As if these people in the house were hungry for this. To hear words of encouragement, something positive, something that gives them hope.

"I want that Chris, I really do." Rachel was sitting in the easy chair turned towards us at the table. I got up and I went to her, bent down and held her hand. She was three months pregnant. "Rachel, you can have a better life. For you and your baby. You still have time. Get out while you can and trust me, once you surrender to Him, He will lift you up and guide you all the way to safety."

Rachel's mom is a heroin addict and we hadn't seen her in quite awhile. Don't even think she knows her own daughter is having a baby. Unfortunately, Rachel got tangled in the same web as her mom. Doing speed balls every chance she gets and still turning tricks while she is pregnant. She's a beautiful girl, and I know she has potential. "Do you really think so Chris?"

Something compelled me to touch her head. I closed my eyes and I felt it. It was like a rush of energy I've never felt before, a pleasantry at best. "Rachel, I believe you will come out of this more than you know." That was the first time I felt a power of that nature. I wasn't quite certain what it was, but for some reason I knew there would be more to come.

Rachel looked at me in awe but not of disbelief as a tear rolled down her cheek. I knew she needed words of encouragement and I hoped that I had given it to her.

I pulled out my sack and went back to the kitchen table. "Yup, I'm done, I have to go home, and my work is finished here." I poured my stones out the sack and there were fourteen stones left. I gave two stones to everyone that was there and said "Here, I won't need these anymore." They all looked at me in disbelief. No one just gives out their dope! I suppose they finally figured out that I wasn't bullshitting them. "Goodbye everyone, I'm leaving and I won't be back. Take care!" And I walked out that door with my head held high and a bounce to my step.

Chapter 25

I finally get it. After all these years of struggling with my addiction and seeking out answers only He could answer, I finally got it. In an instant I realized that there had to be a master plan. His plan for me. In order to do what I needed to do I had to become a part of it. The struggle, the addiction, living on the streets, the dangers, the people. I had to live it, to be a part of it, to lose everything even my dignity to understand the life that people of addiction lived. Then by the grace of God I would come out of it alive, in hopes of bringing testimonial to others seeking solace, redemption and renewed faith in life. This was meant to be. This is the motivation that I needed. This is the driving force to my freedom of bondage. To help others find Jesus and that yes, they too can be renewed!

The Lord is going to take care of me and that's all I needed to live on. A week and a half later I received my tax return. I had quit my job a couple of days ago so I could pack up all my things. My parents were in turmoil over my decision to depart again. Reminding me of the last time I was in Boise. I know they are assuming that they did something wrong for me to take off. But I reassured them that this is for the best and that I have to do this in order to get my life back. I couldn't stay clean living in Seattle. It's too much of a battle. But I told them that I won't be alone. That God will be with me at all times.

My parents finally conceded after telling them this but to put it bluntly as well, I loved them for taking care of me and the kids, but they were also enabling me. They didn't know any other way to deal with my situation so they did what they thought was best. To love me and to support me unconditionally no matter how painful it was to do the things that they didn't want to do.

Chapter 26

Sunday, April 23, 2000.

Today is the conception of the rest of my life. There is no going back, only forward. I handed everything over to God. My trust, my faith and all of my strength comes from knowing that God is my Father. Whatever happens now from this moment on is in His control. He will lead and I shall follow and obey.

As we were going East over the I-90 bridge, I looked in the rear view mirror and I knew that this was for real. I looked at Cord and smiled. "Are you ready son?" He was deep in thought and I wondered if he was thinking of the other night when I found out that he had been skipping school and running off with his friends. The reason for his straight F's in school. I know Cord is a smart kid. His intelligence was visible early in his years. At four years old his favorite shows was the Discovery channel, National Geographic, History channel and Power Rangers. When I attempted college at Highline Community College after Devon and I broke up, which lasted only one semester, Cord came with me to school one day. In my Psychology class my Professor asked a question and no one amongst the students including myself could answer the question. Cord raised his hand and out of curiosity my Professor let him answer. And wouldn't you know it, Cord answered correctly. He was eleven years old. So I know his straight F's came out of nowhere. It was because he was hanging around the wrong kids.

"Ready for what?" Cord asked.

"For our new life in Boise!" I answered.

"Uh, well, I guess." He twisted his head away from me.

"I promised you a better life didn't I? Do you trust me?" I poked him in the rib and he turned to me in defense.

"I don't know why we have to leave Seattle. It's going to suck. But whatever. If you think this is going to make any difference then fine." He turned his attention back to the waters of Puget Sound.

"Well you know, it will do you good starting over too, son. Get your grades up and meet new friends." This move was not only for me as I knew this would benefit him just as well. I wouldn't have forgiven myself if Cord turned out to be anything less of a man. Dealing drugs and becoming a thug was not the future I wanted for him. He has too much potential.

He was bitter, but I was confident that he will come out on top. It's in his character to do so. Someday when he's older and has children of his own he will understand. He will recognize that a mother's love is pure and unconditional. Personally I would be lost and out of control without my kids. Without them I am nothing and I would still be out on the streets of Seattle. I owe them my life and the best thing I can ever give them. To be the mother they deserve. I've been derailed for fifteen years of my existence. I'm ready for a better part of my journey into this thing called life.

One last look in that rear view mirror and the Seattle skyline was fading in the distance. So long, Seattle....here we come Boise!